machine
embroidery

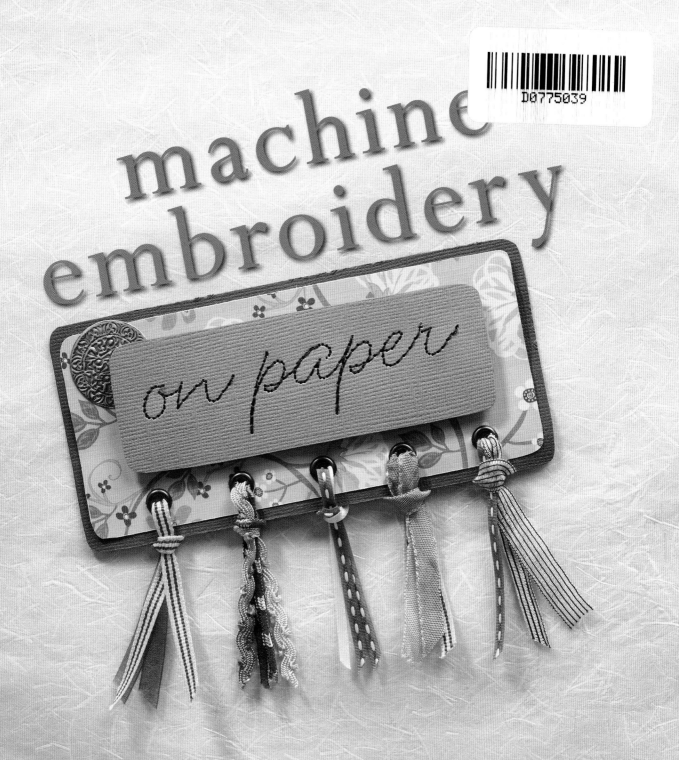

on paper

Annette Gentry Bailey

©2006 Annette Gentry Bailey
Published by

krause publications
An Imprint of F+W Publications

700 East State Street • Iola, WI 54990-0001
715-445-2214 • 888-457-2873

Our toll-free number to place an order or obtain
a free catalog is (800) 258-0929.

The following registered trademark terms and companies appear in this publication:
Baby Lock®; Bazzill Basics Paper™; Bernina®; The C-Thru® Ruler Co.; DMC®; DejaVues®;
Graphic Products Corporation/Black Ink™ Papers; Gorilla Glue®; Husqvarna® Viking®;
Kenmore®; Loose Ends®; Me & My Big Ideas®; Singer®; Sulky®; Waxy Flax™; Windows®.

Library of Congress Catalog Number: 2005935076

ISBN-13: 978-0-89689-302-3
ISBN-10: 0-89689-302-2

Edited by Sarah Brown
Designed by Emily Adler

Printed in China

dedication

I consider myself lucky to have grown up with parents who always supported my creative endeavors. My father told me that when I was 3 years old I took a box of nails and his hammer and pounded them into the ground while he was busy building an addition onto the house. He wasn't the least bit concerned about his nails; instead he got a chuckle out of my wanting to "build" with him. My mother always made sure I had plenty of crayons and paper and a little later on, sewing supplies and any and all craft kits. You name it, I made it: sewing, quilting, hand embroidery, crochet, ceramics, string art, painting, flower arranging, and yes, I even graduated from pounding nails into the dirt to building bird houses and other wood crafts. Somehow, all of this "experience" was leading me to editing, writing and embroidery.

My dad continues to cheer on my accomplishments and I know my mother does the same from heaven. My sister, Heather, and my best girlfriends are always sweetly amazed at what I'm working on. My colleagues-turned-friends are unwaveringly supportive: Linda Griepentrog, Jeanine Twigg and Susan Voigt-Reising. They each know when to offer accolades, encouragement or chocolate—depending on the day and the mood.

And the list wouldn't be complete without my husband, Mark, and my kids Chase and Chandler. My husband has never questioned my work quests in all of the years that we've been married. He has been steadfast in his support of my career and my constant search for the new project. My children, from early ages, understood that mommy works among sewing machines, computer and sketchpad. They inspire me every day and remind me what it's like to look at the world and think that anything is possible.

introduction

When I first discovered I could machine embroider on paper, I must have spent 25 hours just experimenting with different types of papers, stabilizers and designs, looking for the magic combinations that wouldn't tear the paper and distort the designs. That was back when I was planning the first issue of "Paper & Embroidery" magazine (from "Creative Machine Embroidery"). In my mind, scrapbooking and paper projects were a natural place for machine embroidery. Getting the end result just took a little research, but was well worth the effort.

It turns out that paper is a fun and satisfying medium to work with. Thread embellishments take paper to new levels of creativity. This book will show you many techniques and ideas to add machine embroidery to your paper crafts (machine embroidery designs are located on the companion CD-ROM). NOTE: If you do not have an embroidery-capable machine, artwork is included on the CD-ROM so you can create the same designs with traditional sewing machine stitches or by hand with hand-embroidery stitches.

There are more ideas and techniques for embroidery on paper than could possibly fit in one volume. Use the ideas in this book to begin your own journey of discovery to the enjoyment and creativity of embroidering on paper.

table of contents

6 Chapter 1: Embroidery Tool Basics

7 Hoops

7 Needles

7 Threads

8 Stabilizers

8 Sprays

9 Chapter 2: Paper Handling Basics

10 Paper Types

12 Marking Methods

13 Miscellaneous

13 Adhesives

14 Chapter 3: How to Get Started

15 Design Selection

15 Hooping Methods

16 Combining Designs in Software

17 Editing Designs in Software

17 Editing Designs on the Machine Screen

17 Edited Design Legalities

18 Template-Making Methods

18 Embroider On Paper

19 Wording Basics

20 Chapter 4: Scrapbook Tools and Accents

21 Artists' Mediums

21 Beads and Glitter

22 Fabrics

22 Labels, Slides, Tags

23 Metallic Accents

24 Ribbons, Fibers, Trims

24 Stamps

25 Tiles, Stones, Pebbles

25 Zippers, Buttons and Other Sewing Notions

26 Chapter 5: Techniques

27 Edge Finishes

28 Appliqué

32 Beads and Glitter

36 Embossing

37 Folding/Dimension

39 Inks

40 Paints

41 Ribbons and Fibers

43 Tiles, Stones Pebbles

44 Weaving

46 Projects on CD

47 Resources

48 CD-ROM

48 Instructions

48 Contents

CHAPTER 1
Embroidery Tool Basics

1

Once you discover what you can make with paper and embroidery designs, you'll want to dive right in. Before beginning, though, understand what you'll need to get started from the embroidery standpoint. This section will explain hoops, needles, stabilizers and threads. While this book is written for people who have embroidery machines or sewing machines with embroidery capabilities, those who do not have an embroidery machine can use the artwork contained on the CD-ROM as a base for traditional hand embroidery methods or with basic sewing machine stitches.

Hoops

Whether using a stand-alone embroidery machine or a sewing machine with embroidery capabilities, most come with a basic 4" hoop to accommodate designs up to about 3¾" in diameter. Some machine brands also have other sizes available: a smaller hoop, a medium hoop and a much larger hoop. These hoops may be circles, rectangles or other shapes; it all depends on the machine brand. In addition, many companies specialize in making hoops for specific uses. For the best results, always choose the smallest hoop to fit the design.

Check with your local machine dealer to find out which hoop sizes are available for your machine.

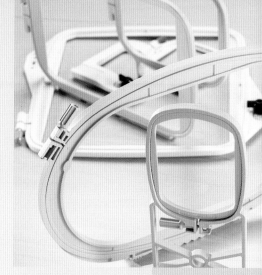

The hoop helps to hold the fabric and stabilizer in place on your machine. It has the same purpose when embroidering paper.

Needles

When embroidering on paper, it's important to use the smallest needle possible, usually a size 65/9, 70/10 or 75/11 (the smaller the number, the smaller the needle). Needle holes are permanent in paper, so the smaller the needle, the smaller the hole.

Threads

Most designs are digitized to use with 40-weight embroidery thread. Rayon threads have a beautiful sheen and are a nice choice for paper projects, however, polyester will work well, too. It is imperative to use threads specifically made for embroidery. The needle penetrates the item being embroidered at a very high rate of speed, and embroidery threads have been manufactured for this purpose. (Keep in mind that the larger the number, the thinner the thread; the smaller the number, the thicker the thread.)

Use bobbin thread in the bobbin unless embroidering something that will show on the back side. Bobbin thread is also specifically manufactured for use with machine embroidery.

Besides rayon thread, several other embroidery threads work well with paper projects:

COTTON: Cotton threads reproduce the look of hand embroidery. Cotton is also a good choice when stitching out freestanding lace designs used as accents on projects. Cotton threads come in different weights, so make sure to test-stitch to see which one works best on your papers.

GLOW-IN-THE-DARK: Expose this thread to light, then turn off the lights and watch it glow. Use it on a Halloween invitation or banner for a fun surprise when it's dark.

METALLIC AND GLITTER: Sparkly thread is a festive choice to highlight areas of designs or for items like holiday cards and party invitations.

Threads from left to right: 40-weight rayon, cotton, twist, metallic, variegated, 12-weight cotton.

TWIST: Like it sounds, twist thread consists of two different threads (usually in two different colors or shades) twisted very tightly together. Generally just a bit thicker, this thread still works well on paper and gives a subtle shaded effect.

VARIEGATED: Variegated threads make a neat striped pattern, affording interest to even the simplest designs.

12-WEIGHT: This is a thicker thread that makes designs really pop. When using it on a paper project, however, be sure to use a heavyweight paper as the base so the stitches won't tear out.

7

Clockwise from top: Tear-away, cut-away and clear water-soluble stablizers.

Stabilizers

A stabilizer is necessary for embroidery. Special stabilizers, from permanents to sprays, are manufactured for this purpose. It's very important to experiment with stabilizers and papers to find what works best, as both come in multiple weight varieties.

CUT-AWAY: This permanent stabilizer stays with the project. Use it with light- to medium-weight papers when show-through is not an issue and for dense designs that will be stitched out and used as appliqués. Cut-away varieties that work well on paper include woven, fusible and mesh. After the design is embroidered, use small, sharp, curved scissors to cut closely around the design. Leave more stabilizer in place if the project edges will not show.

TEAR-AWAY: This temporary stabilizer can be torn away from the design after embroidery. With paper projects, however, it's most desirable to leave it in place or cut it away, as the delicate stitches in paper can easily be pulled out. Tear-away stabilizer is a good choice for medium-weight papers.

WATER-SOLUBLE: This temporary stabilizer rinses out in warm water. Of course, you won't get the papers wet, but there are some instances where you can use clear, water-soluble stabilizer and cut it away. For example, when embroidering on sheer paper, the stabilizer could show through, so using a clear stabilizer is recommended. Cut it away the same as you would a cut-away or tear-away type of stabilizer. Exposing the stabilizer to air for a day or two after embroidery will stiffen it slightly (air dries out water-soluble stabilizers), making it easier to cut away.

Whichever stabilizer you use, remove it carefully, as the papers are delicate. Follow the manufacturer's instructions. Use standard paper scissors to cut around the stabilizer; then use small, sharp, curved scissors to cut near the design. If using tear-away stabilizer, it's still a good idea to use scissors so as not to stress the delicate stitching.

Sprays

Several sprays are available for embroidery use, including spray stabilizers. The spray most often used in conjunction with paper embroidery, however, is temporary spray adhesive. It is used to adhere the paper to the stabilizer. Find more information on temporary spray adhesive on page 16.

CHAPTER 2
Paper Handling Basics

Using paper as a base for embroidery projects is not only possible, but allows creative options that you might not have considered before. This chapter will explain the different types of paper, marking methods and adhesives.

Paper Types

Many papers can be used for embroidery. Knowing the differences between each type will help you select the best one for the project you're working on.

ART: Often handmade, these papers have a high fiber content from threads or added texture from natural particles like leaves, seeds and flowers.

Lightweight art papers.

Medium-weight and heavyweight art papers.

BRITTLE: Vellum, parchment, corrugated and other types with a crisp hand are generally used in scrapbooking for journaling and page accents. Vellum can be machine embroidered when the needle is left un-threaded. It makes a pretty raised outline in the paper (on the wrong side) that can be used as an embellishment.

FABRIC: Available in solids and prints, these fun papers have a combination of fibers that make them useful for paper projects and traditional scrapbooking.

SCRAPBOOK/CARD STOCK: Used for traditional scrapbook layouts and card making, this type of paper is available in every conceivable style and print. It's suitable for backgrounds and accents, but most are not suitable for machine embroidery, as the papers are too lightweight. The exception to this is card stock with a linen blend. This type is just a bit heavier and more flexible than standard card stocks. Always test stitch your card stock choices to find out if they will work with embroidery.

SHEERS: Sheer papers work well as the base for many outline designs. The fine sheer paper must be used with a clear stabilizer and a matching thread in the bobbin so there is no show-through. For items that will be cut out, hoop a double layer of sheer paper and no stabilizer. Always test-stitch first.

SUEDED, FLOCKED, BUBBLE, BAMBOO AND OTHERS: Test first to see how each paper reacts to embroidery. In some cases, ironing a fusible stabilizer to the back first will alleviate any tearing or splitting from the needle. Otherwise, use these specialty papers as backgrounds and accents.

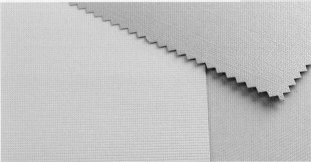
Scrapbook/card stock papers in linen blends.

Sheer papers.

Other papers.

Brittle papers.

Fabric papers.

Scrapbook/card stock papers.

CREDITS
Geometric scrapbook papers from ScrapWorks; seahorse and butterfly scrapbook papers from Bisous.
Blue, purple, swirl, pink, yellow, pink sheer art papers from Loose Ends.
Pink sparkle and cream flocked brittle papers and cream embossed paper from Graphic Products Corporation/Black Ink Papers.
Mauve and dark green medium-weight art papers from The Paper Catalog.
Embroiderable card stock from Bazzill Basics Paper.
All others purchased at paper and scrapbooking stores.

Marking Methods

Traditional fabric marking methods of pens and pins are not appropriate for paper. Use one of the following when marking design placements and choose according to the paper type.

AIR-SOLUBLE MARKERS: Test first on a scrap of paper. If a design will be filled in, it won't matter if any marker remains. Otherwise use one of the other marking methods.

CHALK: Make light marks and then carefully brush away any remaining chalk after embroidery.

REPOSITIONABLE STICKERS: Preprinted with arrows or with space to make a mark in pen or pencil, these are widely available in office supply stores. Stick to mark the spot, line up the design, then peel away.

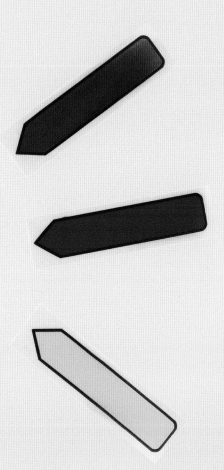

Adhesives

A wide range of adhesives are available for paper crafting. If working with photos, choose an archival-quality type, otherwise choose according to the end result desired.

GLUES

BEADS AND GLITTER: When adding embellishments, choose a glue made specifically for glitter and beads. The glues are often clear drying and can be applied in a thin layer that holds embellishments tightly but without bubbles.

CLEAR: Available in liquid, glue sticks, rubber cement and gun types, clear glues are good for use on items where you don't want any type of show through.

METAL GLUE: Use a glue specifically manufactured for adhering metal to paper when you want a really secure bond for the metal object.

REPOSITIONABLE: This low-tack adhesive allows you to position and reposition without permanence.

WHITE: A multitude of white craft glues are available on the market. Test them on scrap pieces of paper to see which works best.

MOUNTING ADHESIVES

BEAD TAPE: This is a super-sticky double-sided adhesive that comes in rolls or sheets that can be cut to almost any size. Use with micro or seed beads, glitter, sequins, sand or any other fine embellishment.

DOUBLE-SIDED TAPES: When you want to adhere a larger piece of paper, but still like the ease of tapes, a roll of double-sided tape can be cut to any length needed.

GLUE DOTS: Available in different sizes, glue dots adhere pictures, paper and other items, holding them tightly in place. Easy to use, these dots are self-adhesive and come on rolls of paper, making them easy to peel and stick.

GLUE LINES: Similar to glue dots, glue lines are self-adhesive and come on rolls of paper.

POP DOTS: These ⅛"-thick, ½"-diameter circles of foam have self-adhesive backings that allow them to be adhered to paper to lift up an embellishment for more dimension.

PHOTO SQUARES: Flat and double-sided, photo squares come in rolls that peel off for ease in sticking to the back of photos.

Miscellaneous

PAPER SEALER: Paper sealer prevents lightweight papers from warping and bubbling when applying glues or finishes.

SPRAY ADHESIVE: Spray adhesives can be used for a wide range of projects, including paper. Spray adhesives are strong, dry clear and quickly, and usually don't wrinkle, curl or bleed through (except with thin papers). Sprays are available in both permanent and repositionable varieties.

SCISSORS: You'll need some good basic paper-cutting scissors, plus small, curved scissors for cutting out appliqués and cutting close to stitching. In addition, a wide variety of decorative edge scissors are available for paper. They're fun to use for edge finishes or cutting out backgrounds, borders and other shapes.

CHAPTER 3

How to Get Started

Follow the tips in this section for the best success when embroidering on paper. In this chapter, you'll learn how to select appropriate designs for paper projects, hoop the paper, make templates and embroider. Plus, you will get a basic understanding of how to combine and edit designs to make your design library stretch even further.

From top to bottom: Outline design, appliqué design (outline only), chainstitch design, fill design.

Design Selection

The very best designs to use for embroidery on paper are open designs — those without a lot of fill and without underlay stitching (all of the designs featured on the companion CD have been digitized specifically for use on paper). When handled properly with the correct paper and stabilizer choices, however, many designs will work on paper. NOTE: See Chapter 1 for proper stabilizer selection.

- Openwork or outline designs have a minimal stitch count, making them the best choice for papers.
- Quilting or appliqué designs can be used when progressing through only the first set of stitches. Using the satin stitch is not recommended unless using a very fiberous handmade paper or fabric paper with heavy cut-away stabilizer.
- Chainstitch designs work well because of the single stitch needle penetration.
- Fill designs can be used with the best results when stitched directly on heavy cut-away stabilizer. Cut around the design and use it as an appliqué. Fill designs can also be used when altered in embroidery software to remove the underlay stitching and change the stitch density. Embroider on a heavier-weight paper with cut-away stabilizer.

Whatever your choice of papers and motifs, always make sure to embroider a test of the combination first. From the test, you can make design adjustments or choose a different stabilizer before embroidering the final project.

Hooping Methods

Because paper can easily be damaged or permanently wrinkled, it is not hooped. Instead, hoop the stabilizer, spray with temporary adhesive, then adhere the paper to the top. When papers are much larger than the hoop area, roll them up like a carpet and clip with binder clips, clothespins or paperclips on one or both sides (Figure A). Always support the extra weight so the hoop/paper doesn't pull.

TIP
Keep an adhesive remover on hand to easily remove the residue that builds up on hoops.

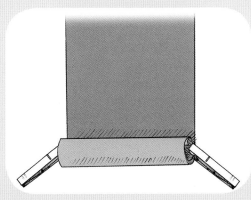

Figure A

Spraying Temporary Adhesive

Place a cardboard box away from your machine to spray temporary adhesives into. Place the hooped stabilizer inside the box and then spray the adhesive onto the stabilizer. Working in this manner will ensure that overspray does not get on, or inside, the machine.

Combining Designs in Software

Embroidery customizing software allows you to combine designs to fit into a larger hoop (a real time saver). For example, combine borders into a longer stitch-out or combine several small designs into one larger design. The following are simple steps; refer to your software manual or visit your local machine dealer for more information.

- Open a blank screen in the software.
- Choose the hoop size you desire to work with.
- Go to the file menu and open the desired designs in the software.
- Use the pointer to move designs or choose from the tool bar (generally there are options to copy, paste, turn vertically and horizontally or move at a 90-degree angle).
- Save the new design combination with a new name.
- Copy to a disk or card, or use whatever method is available to transfer the designs to your machine.

NOTE: See the Design Primer on the companion CD-ROM for design combination suggestions using this book's embroidery designs.

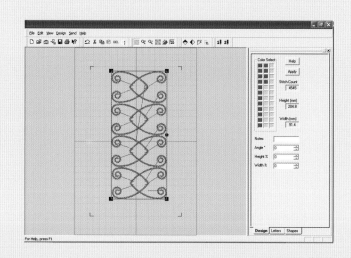

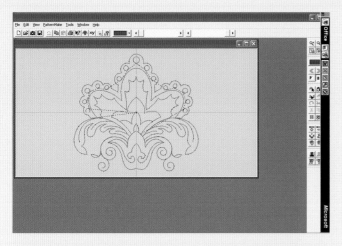

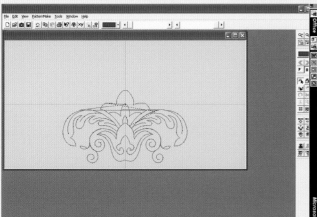

Editing Designs in Software

Another way to get more creative options out of your embroidery design library is by using embroidery editing software. Editing software allows you to use only parts of designs or combine different elements of the same design to make a whole new design. To delete stitches and use part of design:

- Open the software.
- Go to the file menu and open the desired design. Give the design a new name so you don't accidentally alter the original design.
- Use the tool menu to choose the tool that will block out the stitches no longer desired. Use the cutting tool to remove the stitches.
- Use the appropriate tools to change colors, add or delete jump stitches or change the stop commands.

Refer to your software manual or visit your local machine dealer to find out more specific information about editing software and its capabilities.

Edited Design Legalities

Before editing any designs, check with the digitizer or design company and make sure that it is OK to do so. Some digitizing companies and designers do not want their designs altered in any way; others will approve. (The designs included on the companion CD-ROM in this book are OK to edit.)

Under no circumstance can any edited designs be sold as new designs. They are for your personal use only. For more information on copyrighted designs, visit www. embroideryprotection.org.

Editing Designs on the Machine Screen

Some embroidery machines have the capabilities to edit designs on the touch screen. Check your machine manual or visit your local machine dealer to find out more about this process.

Template-Making Methods

Make a template to aid in marking projects using one of the following methods:

- Print a template in software (you may want to change the thread color to black so it shows up well). Position the hoop over the top of the paper template, centering the design. Trace the inside of the hoop and mark the vertical and horizontal cross marks (Figure B).

- Stitch the design onto light cotton fabric. Position the hoop over the top of the fabric, centering the design. Use a thin-line marker to trace the inside of the hoop; mark the vertical and horizontal cross marks.

Figure B

Embroider On Paper

Once the paper, stabilizer, design and thread have been chosen, you're ready to embroider.

1. Make a template of the design using one of the previously mentioned techniques.

2. Mark the design placement on the paper using one of the appropriate methods.

3. Transfer the design to the machine.

4. Hoop the chosen stabilizer and spray with temporary adhesive (place in a box for protection, as described previously under "Spraying Temporary Adhesives"). Adhere the paper to the top of the stabilizer.

5. Attach the hoop to the machine.

Always test-stitch designs before working on the actual project.

6. Embroider a test sample of the design.

7. Remove the hoop from the machine and un-hoop the paper. Check the quality. Make any adjustments necessary.

8. Repeat the steps to embroider the project design.

9. Carefully remove the stabilizer by cutting away.

10. Clip the jump threads.

Wording Basics

Take a cue from the scrapbooking world and add words or phrases to paper projects. This technique, called journaling, can translate well to many other projects besides scrapbook pages.

EMBROIDERED WORDS: The companion CD-ROM in this book contains several digitized words. Use them as a focal point on a page, to describe a loved one's personality or as an added embellishment.

FONTS ON CD: Some companies specialize in creating fonts for use with scrapbooking and paper. The fonts can be loaded on the computer and used just like any other in your word processing program.

HAND-JOURNALING: Give a truly personal touch by hand-lettering a word or phrase or hand writing your own journaling.

PRE-PRINTED: Check your local scrapbooking store for preprinted words, phrases and alphabets in metal, paper and resin and printed on cardstock, velum, rub-on transfers, pebbles, tags, labels, slides and many others. In addition, you can find ribbon and twill tape with printed words and phrases.

WORD PROCESSING PROGRAMS: If you have a basic word processing program, then you probably have a variety of fonts on your desktop ready for use. Use the toolbar to pull down a menu of choices. Change the size of the font as desired. Print on your choice of paper, vellum or card stock.

Embroidered words and alphabets add style to paper projects. Card stock or art papers can be used as the base.

Pre-printed words and alphabets come in every form imaginable from vellum to metal.

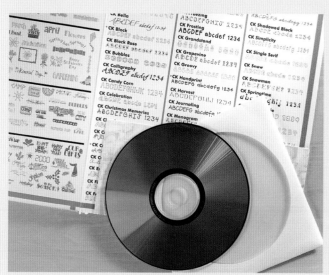

Make your own lettering with a basic word processing program or fonts on CD-ROM.

CREDITS
Alphabet page and vellum phrases from DejaVues, The C-Thru Ruler Co.
Spring Stickers from Bisous.
Woven labels from Me & My Big Ideas.

CHAPTER 4
Scrapbook Tools and Accents

4

Many items traditionally found in scrapbooking stores are making their way into sewing rooms. Familiarize yourself with what's available and incorporate different elements into your paper embroidery projects. You'll notice crossover in many of the categories, thanks to manufacturers' diversity.

Top, from left to right: Chalk, dye, ink. Bottom, from left to right: Marker, paint (metallic), pen (glitter,) pencil.

TIP
Use markers, pencils and paints to fill in the inside of an appliqué embroidery design.

Artists' Mediums

Commonly known as artists' mediums, chalks, dyes, inks, markers, paints, pens and pencils can add drama, whimsy, texture, dimension and so many other effects to paper projects. Practice first on scraps to figure out the looks that appeal to you.

CHALK: Highlight designs for drama by shading around design edges or filling in open areas completely. Chalk comes in numerous color combinations, from earth tones to brights.

DYES: Spritz or sprinkle on papers or moisten handmade papers with a sponge brush to add colors. Let dry thoroughly before using.

INKS: Give papers an old-world look, earthy textures or a wild circus feel. This medium has numerous looks, so have extra scraps on hand to practice with. Inks come in several forms including liquids with needle nose heads and pre-inked stamp pads.

MARKERS: Look for a wide range of tip sizes and colors to add to your supply library. You can write, color, use as accents and more.

PAINTS: No supply library is complete without a variety of paints. Metallic, glitter and basic acrylic colors are just a few that you'll use often.

PENCILS: Colored pencils can add subtle shading to openwork designs and stamps. A charcoal pencil can add sophistication to projects featuring black-and-white photos.

PENS: Like markers, pens are available in a wide range of colors and styles including those with gels and sparkles.

Beads and Glitter

Add sparkle and drama to projects with beads and glitter. They are available in a variety of sizes.

Try This!
- Thread beads on embroidery floss, heavy thread or wire to make tassels. Add sheer ribbons for more interest.
- Hand sew tiny glass beads onto embroidery designs to highlight specific areas. These beads are very subtle, especially when used in tone-on-tone applications. They shimmer in certain lights adding glamour, but don't overpower the look of the design.
- Sew strands of bugle beads down the center of a motif to add sparkle.
- Apply eyelets and thread wire with different sizes of beads; wrap around a project for an easy accent.
- Cut beading tape in the shape desired and sprinkle seed beads over the top.

As with beads, there are also many types of glitter. The finer the glitter type, the better the finished look. While craft glitters will certainly work, they tend to be chunky. Look for very fine art glitters (available at art supply and scrapbooking stores) for the best results.

Try This!
- Use glitter to highlight areas of an embroidery design that you want to emphasize.
- Use a fine tip to apply glue and glitter only to the perimeter of a design.
- Apply glitter to the background paper around a design.
- Use glitter to make add-ons like grass, bugs and wording around embroidery designs.

Fabrics

Fabrics are a natural choice to combine with papers. Many scrapbooking stores offer packs of coordinating fabric. There is even an entire line of fabric papers — 12" square sheets suitable for scrapbooking and many other projects.

Try This!

- Embroider a design, set large eyelets and poke small bits of fabric through the holes.
- Cut cotton chenille strips as accents.
- Use denim or sheer fabric as matting for a photo or embroidery design.
- Embroider a sentiment on linen (fringe the edges for a simple finish) and add to a card front.
- Tear strips of cotton and staple around a card or memory page as a border.

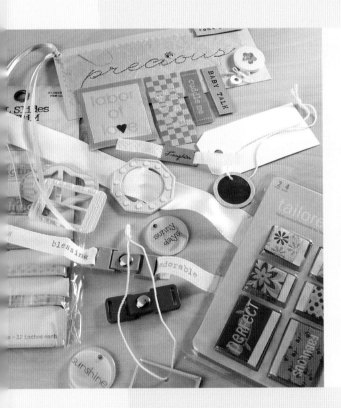

Labels, Slides, Tags

Available in myriad styles, themes and sizes — labels, slides and tags add a fun touch to any paper project. NOTE: Look for instructions on making your own tags on the companion CD-ROM.

Try This!

- Add a series of labels along the edge of a package topper, card or gift box.
- Combine labels and tags for any occasion.
- Find a slide with a descriptive word and hang it from the edge of a photo frame.
- Add tags with numbers to a birthday card.
- Make personalized tags for gift toppers.
- Make several tags and connect them to create a mini book.

CREDITS
Woven labels on card from Me & My Big Ideas.
Loose woven labels from ScrapWorks.
Card stock from Bazzill Basics Paper.

Metallic Accents

Metal accents such as eyelets, charms, corners, mini frames, paper clips and others can be added to projects without a lot of weight and bulk. Sheets and paints are also available to create the look of metals.

Try This!

- Use metal slides on ribbon to hang free from designs.

- Draw attention to a special embroidery motif by placing it inside a miniature frame.

- Connect appliqué letters with charms or rings.

- Connect a series of related embroideries with shaped paper clips.

- Use metal eyelets to hold ribbons, fibers and wires securely to paper.

- Use wires to coordinate with papers.

- Embroider and cut out designs; adhere to a metal sheet as desired and use a dry embossing method to add accents around the designs (see more on dry embossing in Chapter 5).

- Add metal soda caps with rub-on phrases and names to designs.

TIP

Do not use very small accents on projects that children under the age of three will have access to. They are a choking hazard.

Eyelet Setting Tools

Invest in a set of eyelet setting tools to properly place eyelets in all of your paper projects. A basic set might include a punch, eyelet setter and small hammer. A better set might include a needle for piercing papers, different sized punches, eyelet setter and a hammer.

Ribbons, Fibers, Trims

Add texture and interest to any project with the addition of ribbons and fibers. A walk through your local fabric, craft and scrapbooking stores will provide plenty of inspiration.

RIBBONS: Look for ribbons from the sheerest and smallest widths to textured varieties like grosgrain and tapestries in extra-wide styles to add coordinating detail or serve a functional purpose.

FIBERS: Never have fibers and yarns been as popular or abundant as today. Every color imaginable and textures from eyelash to fuzzy can take an ordinary project to extraordinary.

TRIMS: One trip through the home decor department of your local fabric store will yield fabulous trim possibilities from flat braids to beads to feathers and fluff.

Try This!

- Cut out and attach embroidery motifs to the center or ends of ribbons.

- Use a selection of different widths of ribbons and yarns around a hatbox or candle wrap.

- Place flat ribbons on a traditional scrapbook page and then place appliqué embroideries on top for a layered effect.

- Embroider a border on wide ribbon; place in a rectangle, square or oval shape on paper to create a frame.

- Use trims on decorative storage boxes, paper lampshades and candle wraps.

Stamps

Using stamps to accent embroideries is a fun way to add themed details from whimsical to dramatic. Stamps come in a variety of themes, shapes and sizes. You'll find alphabets in many fonts; representation for any and all holidays; seasons, including leaves and florals; abstracts and geometrics; animals; words, phrases and greetings; and many others. They are available in wood, foam, sponge, clear and even a type with interchangeable tops to save space. You can also make your own stamps with objects found around the home like pencil erasers, thread spools and foam hair rollers. Or you can carve custom designs from larger erasers and potatoes.

Try This!

- Use sports stamps and coordinating embroideries on kids' memory pages.

- Stamp a greeting on a card with a companion embroidery motif.

- Stamp a wedding date with embroidered doves and a photo for an anniversary.

- Stamp a background in an allover pattern and then embroider on top of it.

- Use geometric shaped stamps and matching geometric embroidery designs for a textured tone-on-tone look.

Tiles, Stones, Pebbles

Highlight a letter in a word, an entire word or phrase, or use as stand-alone accents on projects. Glass tiles and pebbles come in clear and colored shades. Mosaic glass is available in colors and abstract mixes of colors — all perfect for use on paper projects. You will also find pebbles with words and alphabets.

Try This!

- Spell out a name or word in alphabet pebbles.
- Use colored tiles to create the same shape as a geometric design in a contrasting color.
- Use clear pebbles or tiles over embroideries as accents, such as the center of a flower or certain letters in a word.
- Place large clear tiles over a small photo or embroidery.

Zippers, Buttons and Other Sewing Notions

One trip to your local fabric or scrapbooking store and you can walk away with myriad embellishments for your paper projects.

BUTTONS: Especially interesting, buttons are available in dozens of themes, colors, shapes and sizes.

FUNCTIONAL TYPES: Endless options are available in functional-use products in addition to the obvious ribbons and trims discussed earlier in this chapter. Look for hook-and-eye tape, twill tape, eyelet/grommet tape, button-and-loop tape and many others. Use as clever accents on your projects.

ZIPPERS: Using a zipper on a project is a fun idea, especially for kids. Use self-adhesive zippers especially made for paper, or use cut-to-length sports zippers or standard types in coordinating colors.

ZIPPER PULLS: These decorative add-ons can be used just like charms.

Try This!

- Glue buttons around the lip of a decorative storage box.
- Make a border from zipper tape. Purchase a long sport zipper and cut to the length desired.
- Thread zipper pulls on fibers and use as an accent on a candle wrap or scrapbook page layout.
- Use trims on decorative boxes, paper lampshades, scrapbooking pages and more.

CHAPTER 5
Techniques

The number of techniques that can be used on paper to achieve various finished effects are too numerous for one book. This chapter features several ideas to get you started.

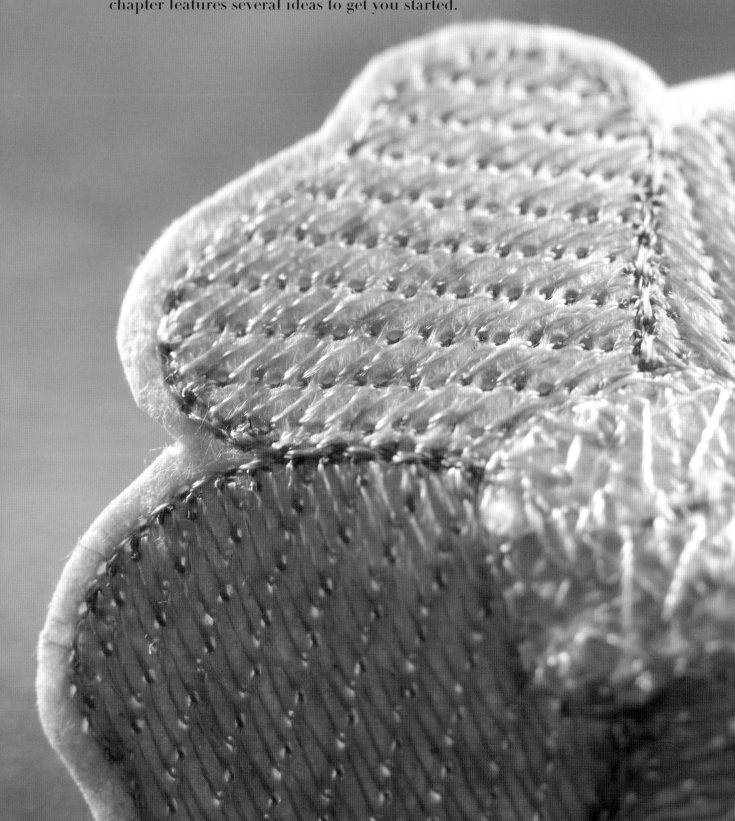

Edge Finishes

Use creative ideas to finish the edges of paper. Here are just a few.

CUTTING: Use decorative-edge scissors or rotary cutting blades to create a quick finished edge on papers. Experiment with different types of scissors and note that some decorative-edge paper scissors will not cut through extra thick papers or fabric papers easily.

EMBROIDERY: Let the design serve as the finished edge on projects. Embroider the chosen motif then trim very closely to the stitching using small, sharp, curved-edge scissors. A satin stitch can give a different finished look than a straight stitch; experiment to see what you like best.

RIBBONS AND FIBERS: Cut, fold and fray ribbons into pretty edge finishes. Some ribbons even come with a self-adhesive backing! Add dimension with fibers textured with sparkles and extra threads.

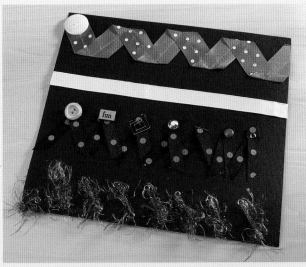

1. Zigzag wide ribbon across paper and straight stitch down the center with monofilament thread to secure.
2. Use self-adhesive ribbon to create a border anywhere.
3. Make loops of ribbon and top with buttons, charms, paper clips, jewels, staples, brads or eyelets.
4. Set eyelets and thread fibers through the holes.

METALS: Metal accents are widely available in different styles and sizes from labels and slides to eyelets and mini frames. Line up multiples in a row to create an edge.

Portable Paper Trimmer

Trimming perfect edges is a breeze when you use a tabletop (portable) paper trimmer. The trimmers are available in various sizes. The basic model fits up to 12" scrapbook papers and the cutting mechanism can easily be replaced when it wears down (it snaps in and out).

TEARING: Torn edges on papers look especially striking. Use the edge of a ruler as a guide or tear freehand. Thicker papers may need to be moistened lightly with the edge of a sponge paintbrush and then torn.

Appliqué

Create different effects with appliqué treatments.

MATERIALS

Medium- and lightweight art papers and card stock

Heavy- and lightweight cut-away and tear-away stabilizer

Temporary spray adhesive

NOTE: These samples feature the FLOWER, FLOWER1 and FLOWER2 embroidery motifs.

TRADITIONAL APPLIQUÉ

Create traditional appliqué much like you would fabric appliqué.

1. Hoop tear-away stabilizer, spray with temporary adhesive and attach the paper desired for the background.

2. Place another color paper on top of the background paper. Embroider the first part of the design.

3. Remove the hoop, but do not un-hoop the papers. Use small, sharp, curved scissors to carefully cut around the motif up to, but not through, the stitching lines (Figure A).

4. Place the hoop back on the machine. Place the next color of paper, if applicable. Embroider the design.

5. Repeat Step 3. Continue in the same manner until the design is complete.

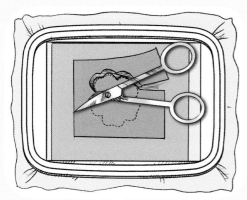

Figure A

HEAVY FILL APPLIQUÉ

Traditional fill embroidery designs can often have too high a stitch count to successfully stitch on paper. Instead, handle this type of appliqué as follows:

1. Hoop heavy cut-away stabilizer.

2. Place the hoop on the machine.

3. Embroider the design.

4. Remove the hoop. Un-hoop the design and carefully cut around the design using small, sharp, curved scissors.

5. If the stabilizer shows along the edges, use markers to match the thread colors and cover the stabilizer.

TIP

If the design begins to pucker, remove the hoop and add a rectangle of cut-away stabilizer to the back (lightly spray with temporary adhesive to adhere).

LIGHT FILL APPLIQUÉ

A light fill appliqué is a design that has no underlay stitching, but still has stitching that sparsely covers the paper.

1. Hoop lightweight cut-away stabilizer.

2. Spray with temporary adhesive and attach the paper.

3. Embroider the design.

4. Remove the hoop. Un-hoop the design and cut away most of the stabilizer.

5. If desired, use small, sharp, curved scissors to carefully cut outside the design, leaving a narrow border of paper.

◀ This light fill appliqué sample is embroidered on card stock. The stitching is a contrast to the paper.

◀ This light fill appliqué sample is embroidered on handmade paper. Notice the texture and add-ins show through.

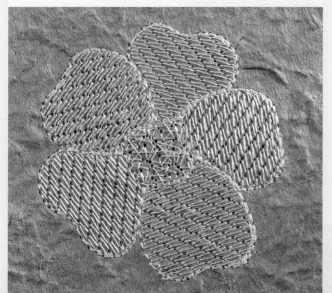

REVERSE APPLIQUÉ

With this appliqué method, the background papers are allowed to show through in the design. This method is not recommended for very small areas, as it is too hard to cut away the paper.

1. Hoop tear-away stabilizer, spray with temporary adhesive and attach the paper desired to show through in the design.

2. Place the next paper on top of the first layer. Spray the upper area of the paper with temporary adhesive and lightly adhere. Do NOT spray over the design area, as the papers need to cut apart easily.

3. Place the hoop on the machine.

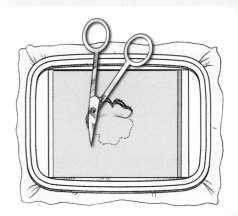

Figure B

4. Embroider the design.

5. Remove the hoop, but do not un-hoop the papers.

6. Use small, sharp, curved scissors to carefully cut around the motif inside the stitching lines (Figure B). Cut through ONLY the top paper layer, leaving the bottom paper to show through in the design.

7. Repeat this process until the design is complete. Note that in this flower sample, the center was too small to cut out so another piece of paper was placed over the top center, embroidered and then cut around after all the other embroidery and paper cutting was complete.

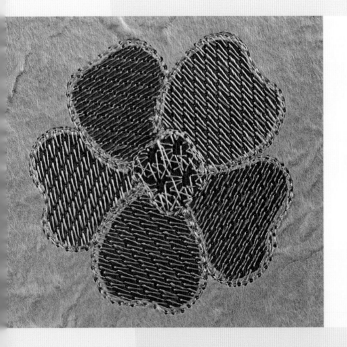

REVERSE APPLIQUÉ WITH FILL

This technique takes reverse appliqué one step further with pretty fill stitching on the base paper.

1. Follow the first three steps of Reverse Appliqué.

2. Embroider the outline design. Remove the hoop from the machine, but do not un-hoop.

3. Use small, sharp, curved scissors to carefully cut around the motif inside the stitching lines. Cut through only the top paper layer, leaving the bottom paper to show through the design.

4. Place the hoop back on the machine; this time, embroider the fill design. The stitching will cover the background paper to shade it. Use a contrasting color of thread to best show off the stitching.

RAGGY EDGE APPLIQUÉ

Similar to the raggy edge technique found in quilting, raggy edge paper appliqué adds a country touch to projects.

1. Choose two different colors of medium-weight art paper.

2. Hoop tear-away stabilizer, spray with temporary adhesive and adhere the color chosen for the embroidery background to the stabilizer.

3. Print out a template of the chosen design. Add ¼" all around the outside of the design. Cut out the design template.

4. Trace the design onto the back of the paper chosen for the appliqué.

5. Cut out the art paper design carefully.

6. Transfer the design to the machine.

7. Embroider the outline of the design for placement.

8. Place the art paper design on top of the placement lines. Restart the design and embroider the center or the remainder of the design.

9. Un-hoop and remove the stabilizer.

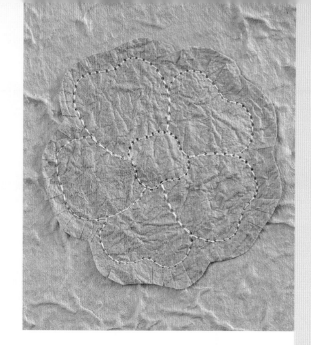

10. Use small, sharp scissors to clip the edge of the design to, but not through, the stitching line. Fold the ragged edges up with your fingertips.

DIMENSIONAL APPLIQUÉ

Just like the name implies, dimensional appliqué is raised above the background paper.

1. Choose at least five lightweight (tissue-weight) art papers and one medium- to heavyweight background paper.

2. Choose a design such as this flower that has an outline and detail in the middle that will hold the papers in place.

3. Make a template of the design.

4. Place the template pattern over the layers of paper and cut around the design (Figure C).

5. Hoop the stabilizer, spray with temporary adhesive and adhere the background paper.

6. Transfer the design to the machine.

7. Embroider the design outline only.

8. Place the layers of paper over the outline. NOTE: If desired, you can lightly spray the centers with temporary adhesive to hold them together.

9. Embroider the center element. Un-hoop and remove the stabilizer.

10. Peel the layers of paper apart and finger-press them up and around the center to give them their dimension.

NOTE: See more on adding dimension to papers under Folding/Dimension on page 37.

Figure C

Tip
Use different colors of paper for more interest.

Beads and Glitter

There's no better way to add splash to embroidery designs than with beads and glitter. Use these ideas as a jumping-off point, then create some of your own.

GENERAL MATERIALS
- Beads in different sizes including micro beads, glass beads, seed beads, large eye beads, decorative shapes, etc.
- Hand beading needle
- Hand sewing needle
- Monofilament and 12-weight thread
- Beading tape
- Fine-gauge beading wire
- Eyelets and appropriate setting tools
- Clear-drying glue
- Fine art glitter and other glitter types as desired
- Fine bristle paintbrush
- Paper plates

Beads

Once you begin experimenting with beads, you'll discover more and more ways to use them in your paper projects.

DIMENSIONAL DESIGN AND BEADS
This technique fools the eye with a 3-D look.

1. Prepare the hoop using the stabilizer appropriate for the paper chosen and transfer the design to the machine.

2. Embroider the desired design onto the paper (the sample features the LBORDER2 embroidery motif).

3. Embroider only the leaves onto another piece of art paper (skip past the vine stitching).

4. Cut out the leaves next to the stitching lines and hand stitch them over their respective mate on the main design.

5. Use a hand beading needle, monofilament thread and seed beads to highlight the portions of the embroidery design desired. NOTE: The sample shown features beading along the vine only.

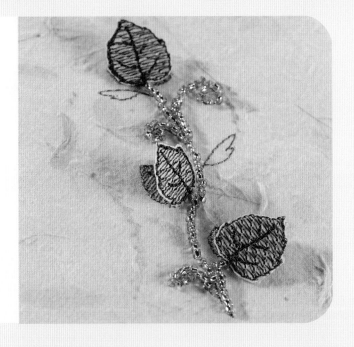

BEADING TAPE
Create a unique border by alternating an embroidered design and the same design covered in beads.

1. Print out the template desired. Cut out the design.

2. Trace it on the top of the beading tape (over the paper side). Cut out the design.

3. Peel away the paper to reveal the adhesive. Adhere to the surface desired.

4. Peel away the second layer of paper and sprinkle beads over the top of the tape. Lightly press with your fingertips.

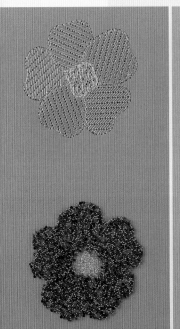
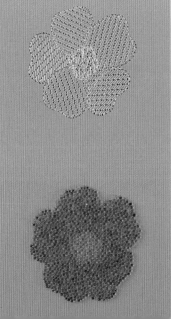

◀ Beading tape is a heavy-duty double-sided tape. The bottom side adheres to the surface of the project while the top holds the beads firmly in place. These samples show micro beads at right and Beadazzles with a glitter center at left.

BEADED WIRE BORDER

Beading and wire can make a unique focal point for embroidery designs.

1. Use software and a larger hoop to create a border design. The sample features the SBORDER2 embroidery motif turned and mirror imaged with space in between for the beading.

2. Transfer the designs to the machine.

3. Hoop stabilizer, spray with temporary adhesive and adhere with the art paper of your choice.

4. Embroider the designs. Remove the stabilizer.

5. Apply eyelets at the end of each design, following the manufacturer's directions.

6. Cut fine gauge wire and thread with beads. Run each end through the eyelets and twist the ends into a knot. Place masking tape over the top of the knot for extra security.

EMBROIDERY AND PARTIAL BEADED FILL

This easy idea highlights just one area of a design with beading.

1. Transfer the design of your choice to the machine. This sample features the TURTLE2 embroidery motif.

2. Prepare the hoop using the stabilizer appropriate for the paper chosen. Hold in place with temporary adhesive.

3. Embroider the design, skipping past part of the stitching to leave it open. In the turtle sample, Color 4 was skipped to leave the shell open.

4. Use a small paintbrush and clear drying glue to fill in the shell inside the stitching lines. Sprinkle super-fine beads or sequins such as Beadazzles until the glue is covered. Let dry.

This sample features a fun mix of both embroidery and beading. The beading is actually made from a sequins material. It's just right for this application.

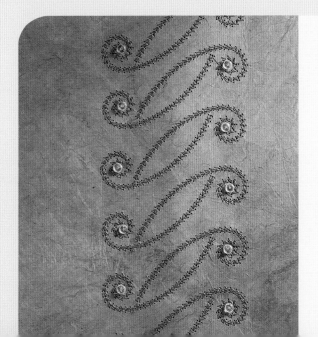

SINGLE BEADS

Nest single beads inside embroidery designs for subtlety.

1. Use software and a larger hoop to create a border design. This sample features the SBORDER2 embroidery motif turned and mirror imaged to create small curls at each side. It's then repeated to create a larger border design.

2. Transfer the design to the machine.

3. Prepare the hoop using the stabilizer appropriate for the paper chosen. Hold in place with temporary adhesive.

4. Embroider the border. Remove the stabilizer.

5. Hand sew flat, medium-sized beads inside each curl using a hand beading needle and monofilament thread.

BEAD FRINGE

Create a quick beaded fringe that hangs free from the embroidery design.

1. Use software and a larger hoop to create a border design. This sample features the SCORNER1 embroidery motif turned and lined up in a row.

2. Transfer the design to the machine.

3. Prepare the hoop using the stabilizer appropriate for the paper chosen. Hold in place with temporary adhesive.

4. Embroider the design using 12-weight thread. Repeat over the first stitching. Remove the stabilizer.

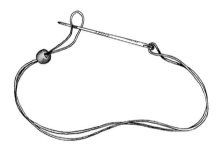

Figure D

5. Thread a hand sewing needle with 12-weight thread; knot the double strand.

6. Pick up a large-eye bead and thread it on the needle; thread the needle through the knotted end (Figure D).

7. Pick up the desired number of beads and poke the needle through the fabric at the end of the design. Knot on the back side to secure the strand.

Glitter
Glitter can change the look of a project with one shake.

GLITTER FILL

Fill in outline embroidery designs with matching glitter colors. NOTE: For full instructions of the sample pictured, see the companion CD-ROM.

1. Prepare the hoop using the stabilizer appropriate for the paper chosen. Embroider the desired design.

2. Use a fine bristle paintbrush to apply clear-drying glue inside the stitching lines.

3. Sprinkle fine art glitter inside the design. In the sample, glitter colors were matched to the embroidery thread colors. Work over a paper plate when applying the glitter. Save the excess glitter for reuse.

GLITTER PAINT OVER APPLIQUÉ

For the times when you want a design to jump out, apply glitter paint over the entire area. NOTE: For full instructions on the sample pictured, see the companion CD-ROM.

GLITTER RUB

For an overall sparkling effect, create a glitter rub over a finished embroidered background.

1. Prepare the hoop using the stabilizer appropriate for the paper chosen. NOTE: Fine art glitter sticks best on very textured art papers. Embroider the desired design.

2. Sprinkle fine art glitter lightly over the background and use your fingertips to rub it around and into the texture of the paper.

3. Turn the paper upside down over a paper plate and tap the sides to remove the excess glitter.

Mica Flakes

Sparkly like glitter, but chunkier, mica flakes are non-tarnishing natural pieces of mica. Use them as a fill like this sample, or in small accent areas. This sample features the SBORDER1 embroidery design turned and mirror imaged to create an abstract box. Apply clear-drying glue with a fine bristle paintbrush slightly inside the stitching lines, then sprinkle mica flakes over the glue. Press lightly with fingertips to adhere. Let dry.

CREDITS
Beadazzles from Ranger Industries.
Card stock from Bazzill Basics Paper.
Fabric paper from Michael Miller Memories.

Embossing

Both dry and heat embossing are fun techniques that add unique features to embroidered designs.

MATERIALS
- Art papers and card stock
- Embossing stencils
- Embossing tool
- Light box
- Stamps
- Pigment ink
- Embossing powder
- Heat embossing tool

Counter-clockwise from left: This Fall card features embossed leaves around the outside edge. The tag features a different technique: embossed miniature flowers are cut out of card stock, grouped and adhered at the edge of the embroidered tag. The embossed frame highlights a ladybug embroidery motif while the embossed dots highlight the background.

DRY EMBOSSING

To add a raised surface to papers, use the dry embossing technique. NOTE: For full instructions to make the tag and card pictured, see the companion CD-ROM.

1. Choose the stencil and card stock or art paper colors desired.

2. Place the stencil on the light box and the card stock right-side down over the stencil.

3. Use the embossing tool to rub the paper into shape (Figure E). Repeat as needed to create the shapes.

4. Use small, sharp scissors to cut out the shapes and apply glue to hold them in place on the project (or create them directly on a paper that is used as the background for a project).

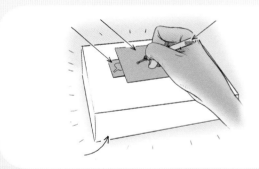

Figure E

Try This!

Look for embossing stencils where you can replace one element with embroidery, such as this sample. The stencil has a half-flower along with the pumpkin and ladybug. The complete stencil was embossed except for the flower petals. In place of the embossed petals, embroidered ones were made on card stock, then individually cut out and glued in place where the embossed petals would have been. The dimensional aspect of the paper is intact, but the embroidery adds an unexpected element.

HEAT EMBOSSING

Another fun — and easy — effect is to use a heat embossing technique on papers.

1. Choose the paper desired for embossing.

2. Coat the stamp with pigment ink. Press the stamp onto the paper. Or use a pigment pen to fill in part of a design.

3. Coat the wet ink with embossing powder (place a paper plate underneath to catch the excess powder).

4. Use the heat tool to set the embossing powder.

◀ Top and bottom: Embroider an openwork design on ready-made dry embossed paper or another art paper; then use a clear embossing pen and sparkly embossing powder to fill in part of the design.
Center: Create an allover background, then use an outline embroidery design over the top.

Folding/Dimension

Add dimension to paper projects with easy folding and layering techniques.

ACCORDION FOLDS

Create easy accordion folds for an interesting scrapbook accent or use it on a larger scale like a decorative fireplace fan or wall décor. NOTE: For complete instructions on making the Decorative Fireplace Fan, see the companion CD-ROM.

MATERIALS
• Medium-weight textured art paper
• Fusible interfacing
• Firm ruler
NOTE: For the purposes of testing the technique, use a rectangle of paper approximately 10" x 14".

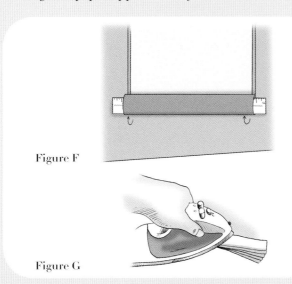

Figure F

Figure G

1. Cut the interfacing slightly smaller than the rectangle of paper. Fuse it to the back of the art paper, following the manufacturer's directions.

2. Place the ruler on the wrong side of the paper; fold the paper over the ruler and finger press (Figure F). Turn the paper to the front and repeat.

3. Continue in a back-and-forth manner until the rectangle is folded.

4. Turn the creased paper to the wrong side and use the iron to firmly press the creases in place (Figure G).

TRI-FOLD BOOK

Use this little book alone or as an accent on a scrapbook page.

MATERIALS

NOTE: The materials listed are to create the book base only. For complete instructions on the project shown, see the companion CD-ROM.

- 12" x 12" sheet of scrapbook paper
- Scraps of card stock
- 2 eyelets and appropriate setting tools
- Waxed thread or embroidery floss
- Ruler
- Scissors
- Optional: Sheer fabric, circle cutter

TIP

Use the book to record sentiments, keep photos or journal an event.

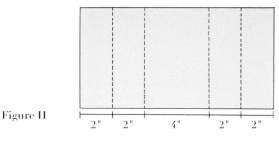

Figure H

2" 2" 4" 2" 2"

Figure I

3" 3"

1. Cut a 6¼" x 12" rectangle of scrapbook paper. NOTE: Make your booklet shorter or taller as desired.

2. Cut a 5¾" x 11¾" piece of sheer paper. Adhere to the inside with clear drying glue or vellum tape.

3. Follow the diagram to fold (Figure H). Use the ruler as a guide to make straight edges.

4. Cut two 3/4"-diameter circles from card stock or use a circle cutter.

5. Unfold the book and mark the circle placements as shown on the right side (Figure I).

6. Apply the eyelets to each circle using the appropriate setting tools, making sure they go through the scrapbook paper and fabric layers.

7. Refold the book and twist a length of waxed thread or floss around the circle closures.

FREESTANDING LAYERED FLOWER

Use this pretty flower as a single accent, group into a border or hang from ribbons.

MATERIALS

Sheer art papers
Embroidery thread
Petal embroidery design

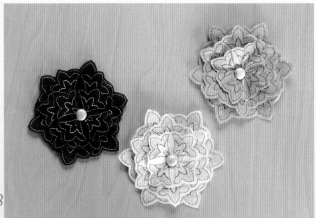

1. Create a four-petal and six-petal flower in software. Copy and enlarge one six-petal flower 20 percent. NOTE: The sample petals were created in editing software from the FLORAL design and saved with a new name.

2. Cut two rectangles of sheer art paper larger than the hoop. Hoop both papers WITHOUT stabilizer. NOTE: Because the flower will be cut out around the design, it doesn't matter if the paper is hooped (and creased at the hoop edges).

3. Wind a bobbin with the same thread as the needle.

4. Embroider one four-petal design. Un-hoop. Repeat to embroider two six-petal designs.

5. Use small, sharp scissors to carefully cut around the designs.

6. Stack the layers with the largest on the bottom (turning one layer slightly to off-set the next layer) and the four-petal flower on top. Hold the layers together with a brad in the center.

7. Pinch the layers around the brad to make them stand up.

Inks

Working with inks is a quick and easy way to create unique backgrounds and focal points.

GENERAL MATERIALS
- Card stock and art papers as desired
- Liquid inks with needle nose head, inked stamp pad
- Firm sponge

STRIPED INK ON CARD STOCK

1. Working with ink from needle nose bottles and a firm sponge, choose three colors and carefully apply to one end of the sponge (Figure J).
2. Brush the sponge across the card stock from left to right, repeating to create rows. Reapply ink if needed. Let dry.
3. Embroider as usual.

Figure J

SPONGE INKING

1. Ink one end of a sponge and press down over art paper in a random pattern. Press firmly in some areas and lightly in others to vary the depth of ink.
2. Repeat with a second color on the opposite end of the sponge. Let dry.
3. Embroider as usual.

BRUSHED INK ON ART PAPER

1. Choose a highly textured art paper.
2. Apply ink from a needle nose bottle to one short end of a sponge.
3. Brush the inked side lightly over the top of the paper. The ink applied to raised areas shows in a darker shade than the indented areas, creating focused dimension. Let dry.
4. Embroider as usual.

INK PAD STAMPING

1. Prepare the intended embroidery. This sample features the SBORDER1 embroidery motif repeated three times and turned to create the tails on shooting stars; it was stitched in metallic thread for sparkle.
2. Press the stamp over the ink pad to completely cover the top of the stamp. This sample features metallic ink.
3. Press the inked stamp firmly on the paper. Repeat until the desired number of stamps are complete.

CREDITS
Liquid Inks from Ranger Industries.
Card stock from Bazzill Basics Paper.
Blue art paper from Loose Ends.

Paints

Paints can be used in several ways to enhance embroidery.

GENERAL MATERIALS

- Card stock and art papers as desired
- Selection of acrylic, metallic, pearl or glitter paints
- Paintbrushes in several sizes (for different affects)
- Stamp of your choice

STAMPED BACKGROUND

Create your own background with metallic paint and a stamp.

1. Choose a paper for the embroidery background. Any type except tissue paper will work.

2. Use the stamp of your choice to create an allover design. Choose an abstract stamp such as a geometric design so that it enhances, rather than overpowers, the embroidery.

3. Use a fine bristle paintbrush to brush paint over the top of the stamp. Do not overload the stamp with paint.

4. Press down firmly on the paper; move to a new spot and press again. Reload the stamp with paint and continue until the paper is filled as desired. Let dry.

5. Embroider the design over the top of the paper as you would another paper of the same weight.

SPRAYED BACKGROUND

Glitter spray paint goes on easily and gives a background sparkle for any embroidery. This sample features an embroidered shadow effect.

1. Choose a design with an outline only. Enlarge it 20 percent in software or at the touch screen of the machine. Prepare the hoop for card stock and embroider a design. Un-hoop.

2. Prepare another hoop for card stock. Embroider the design again, this time with the fill and at the regular size.

3. Spray glitter paint (outside and on newspapers) over the outline design and paper. Let dry.

4. Use small, sharp scissors to cut around the fill design, leaving a small border of paper.

5. Place the fill over the outline. Use pop dots or small squares of mounting tape behind the design so it's raised off the surface of the outline design and background paper.

6. Add other embellishments as desired.

TIP
Test paints on scraps of paper first. Some have a higher water content and can warp paper.

PAINT FILL

Use paint to fill in all or part of an embroidery design.

1. Prepare a hoop with the stabilizer appropriate for the chosen paper. Embroider an openwork design.

2. Un-hoop and remove the stabilizer.

3. Use a small paintbrush and the paints of your choice to carefully paint inside the stitching lines. Do not overload the paintbrush with paint. Let dry.

Ribbons and Fibers

Adding ribbons and fibers to paper projects gives them personality. From functional to purely decorative, there is no end to how you can manipulate and use ribbons and fibers.

GENERAL MATERIALS
- Ribbons and fibers
- Sharp scissors
- Embellishments as desired, such as buttons, beads, wire, eyelets and appropriate setting tools, etc.
- Glue
- Scissors

DANGLING DESIGNS

Embroider designs to hang on ribbon for a garland, mobile, ornament and more.

1. Use software to make several sets of designs. This sample features the CCANE embroidery motif, mirror imaging one of each set. Use a larger hoop if available. Otherwise, mirror image on screen and re-hoop as needed to complete a set.

2. Prepare the hoop for embroidery using the stabilizer appropriate for the paper chosen. Embroider the designs.

3. Remove the hoop and un-hoop the designs.

4. Use small, sharp scissors to carefully cut around the designs just outside the stitching lines.

5. Sandwich your choice of ribbon(s) between sets of designs and glue in place.

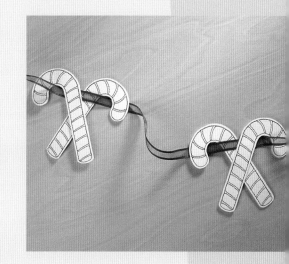

TIP
Highlight areas of the design with paint or glitter or otherwise embellish the embroideries, if desired.

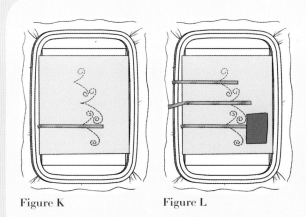

Figure K   Figure L

FLOWER STEMS

Create the look of flowers dancing in the wind by using ribbon as the flower stem.

1. Use a small flower or capture an element like the tulip from the larger FLORAL motif in editing software to create the appliqué. Save the designs with a new name. Turn the SBORDER1 in software and mirror image it to create the look of leaves. Group several using the software. Change the size, if desired (the yellow tulip in the sample was reduced 20 percent). Transfer the designs to the machine.

2. Hoop the appropriate stabilizer for the paper desired.

3. Make a template and mark the design placement.

4. Place a piece of ribbon under the first stem and embroider (the leaves will stitch off the ribbon). Repeat for more stems/leaves if desired (Figure K).

5. Place a square of paper over the intended flower and embroider the design, making sure the end of the stem is tucked underneath (Figure L).

6. Use small, sharp, curved scissors to cut around the appliqué, leaving a small border. Repeat for other flowers as desired.

7. Turn the end of the stem lower edge under; create a loop or trim even to finish. Embellish with bug buttons.

FIBER TAILS

Metal eyelets and fibers combine for an application with lots of texture.

1. Prepare the hoop for embroidery using the stabilizer appropriate for the paper chosen.

2. Embroider the design of your choice. This sample features the SBORDER2 embroidery motif turned and repeated.

3. Apply eyelets following the manufacturer's directions in the arrangement desired.

4. Thread a selection of fibers through the hole and knot to secure. Cut the ends even.

TIP
Look for coordinating sets of fibers available in fabric and scrapbooking stores.

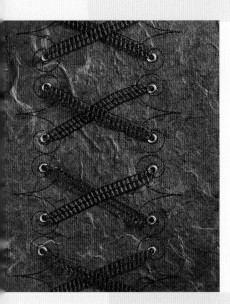

LACING

Just like lacing up a shoe, you can create a unique border with pretty fibers.

1. Prepare the hoop for embroidery using the stabilizer appropriate for the paper chosen.

2. Embroider a design that can be embellished with eyelets. Use editing software and a larger hoop to create a border. Save the design with a new name. This sample features the SCORNER1 embroidery motif turned outward and repeated.

3. Apply coordinating eyelets following the manufacturer's directions in the arrangement desired.

4. Thread ribbon through the eyelets in the same manner you would lace up a shoe. Tie in a knot at the back.

SHEER KNOTS

This sample showcases sheer ribbon.

1. Prepare the hoop for embroidery using stabilizer appropriate for the paper chosen.

2. Embroider a design that can be embellished with eyelets. Use software and a larger hoop to create a border. Save the design with a new name. This sample features the SBORDER2 embroidery motif turned, mirrored and repeated.

3. Un-hoop. Apply eyelets following the manufacturer's directions.

4. Thread sheer ribbon through the eyelets; tie in a knot and clip the ends at an angle.

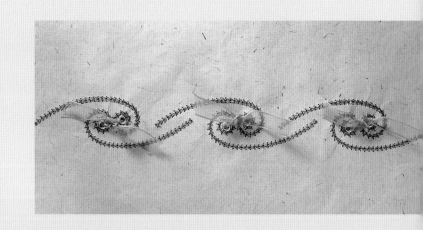

Tiles, Stones, Pebbles

Tiles, stones and pebbles are quick and easy embellishments to add to embroidered designs.

MOSAIC TILES

1. Prepare the hoop for embroidery using the stabilizer appropriate for the paper chosen.

2. Embroider a design such as the ALLOVER motif and repeat the number of times desired, leaving space in between each design for the tiles.

3. Un-hoop. Alternate colored mosaic tiles in the pattern of your choice between the designs. Glue in place.

STONE ACCENTS

1. Prepare the hoop for embroidery using the stabilizer appropriate for the paper chosen.

2. Embroider the desired design. The green sample features the FLORAL embroidery motif; the blue sample features the SCORNER1 embroidery motif turned and mirrored in software.

3. Un-hoop. Add the stones using one of the following options:

- Use heat-adhesive rhinestones and the appropriate applicator tool to set the rhinestones in place (as shown in the green sample). NOTE: The featured design has small circles that were used as placement marks for the rhinestones.

- Use clear-drying glue and tweezers to place the stones on the paper.

FLOWER CENTERS

1. Prepare the hoop for embroidery using the stabilizer appropriate for the paper chosen.

2. Choose a flower motif or make your own by capturing a single element from a larger design in editing software and repeating it to create petals. Save the design with a new name.

3. Embroider the design. Un-hoop and adhere the pebble or stone desired to the center.

PEBBLE WORDING

1. Prepare the hoop for embroidery using the stabilizer appropriate for the paper chosen.

2. Embroider the word of your choice. Un-hoop.

3. Use self-adhesive pebble alphabet letters to spell out additional words to complement the design. The sample features coordinating alphabet letters in different sizes for whimsy.

CREDITS

Light blue paper from Loose Ends. Green paper from The Paper Catalog.
Rhinestones and heat setting tool from Oklahoma Embroidery Supply & Design.

Weaving

Weaving papers or other mediums creates an interesting background for embroidery.

GENERAL MATERIALS
- Art paper and fabric paper
- Flat ribbon between ¼"- and ⅜"-wide
- Paper-release adhesive stabilizer
- Craft knife
- Cutting mat or other safe surface
- Ruler
- Pencil

WEAVING WITH RIBBON

Use flat ribbon and lightweight paper strips to create this background.

1. Cut strips of paper and lengths of ribbon slightly longer than the hoop.

2. Cut a piece of paper-release adhesive stabilizer larger than the hoop. Peel away a 3¾" section of the paper in the middle.

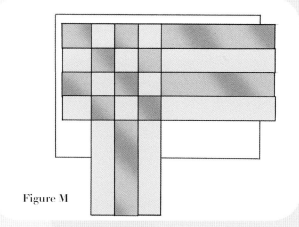

Figure M

3. Begin at one corner and carefully weave the paper and ribbon strips together, pressing them gently to the adhesive (Figure M). Alternate a paper and ribbon each time until the area is completely filled.

4. Hoop the stabilizer, being careful not to catch the paper inside the hoop. Embroider the design of your choice over the top.

NOTE: To make a larger background, use longer paper strips and a larger piece of adhesive stabilizer. To embroider, hoop a piece of tear-away stabilizer, spray with temporary adhesive and adhere the woven piece on top. This will ensure that the paper stays intact through the embroidery process.

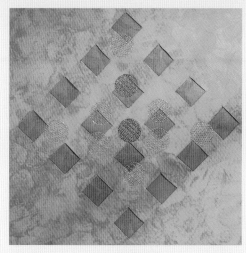

DIAGONAL TWO COLOR

Slits cut on the diagonal of fabric paper, threaded with a contrasting color and embroidered with polka dots make for a graphic combination.

1. On the wrong side of the fabric paper, mark diagonal lines 1" apart across the length of the fabric (Figure N).

2. On a cutting mat or protected surface, use the craft knife to cut 1"-long marks along the length of each line (Figure O).

3. Cut ⅞"-wide strips of a contrasting color fabric paper.

4. Thread the strips through the 1"-wide slits (Figure P).

5. Hoop tear-away stabilizer, spray with temporary adhesive and adhere the woven fabric to the center.

6. Embroider the design(s) of your choice. This sample shows a combination of PolkaDots1, 2 and 3 randomly combined in software and stitched in a larger hoop.

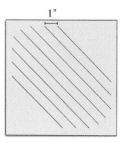

Figure N

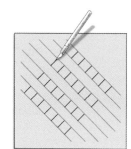

Figure O

Figure P

DIAMOND WEAVE

A more advanced technique, the diamond weave is a good background for wording.

1. Cut strips of two contrasting colors of fabric paper between ⅞" and 1" wide.

2. Beginning with two contrasting strips, make an "X" (Figure Q).

3. Add another strip to either side (Figure R).

4. Place a piece of self-adhesive stabilizer behind the strips to help hold them in place. Do not press down until the strip is exactly placed.

5. Continue placing strips in the same manner until the weaving is the size desired.

6. Stitch around the edges in sewing mode to hold the weave permanently in place.

7. Hoop cut-away stabilizer, spray with temporary adhesive and adhere the woven fabric in place. Embroider as usual.

CREDITS
Pink and green paper from The Paper Catalog.
Fabric paper from Michael Miller.
Pink stripe paper from Loose Ends.

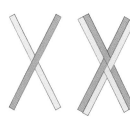

Figure Q   Figure R

Projects on CD

Step-by-step instructions for these projects can be found on the companion CD-ROM.

Greeting Cards

Picture Frames

Wall Art

Decorative Fireplace Fan

Tags

Hat Boxes

Candle Wraps

"Darling"
Scrapbook Page Layout

Mirror

Sachets

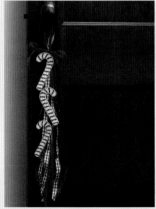
Holiday Door Jinglers

"Fun, Fun, Fun"
Scrapbook Page Layout

resources

The following companies were generous enough to donate many of the products found in this book. All others were purchased at retail outlets. For information on embroidery machines and sewing machines with embroidery capabilities, visit your local dealer or the manufacturer's Web site.

Baby Lock
(800) 422-2953
www.babylock.com

Bazzill Basics Paper
Available at your local craft or scrapbook store or from a number of online retailers.
www.bazzillbasics.com

Beacon Adhesives
www.beaconcreates.com

Bernina
(800) 669-1647
www.berninausa.com

Bisous
www.bisous.biz

Brother
(800) 422-7684
www.brother.com

The C-Thru Ruler Company (Deja Views)
www.cthruruler.com

DMC
www.dmc-usa.com

Elna USA
(800) 848-3562
www.elnausa.com

Floriani Embroidery Products
(865) 426-2685
www.RNKDistributing.com

Graphic Products Corporation/Black Ink Papers
(800) 323-1658 (ask for the dealer nearest you)
www.gpcpapers.com

The Gorilla Glue Company
(800) 966-3458
www.gorillaglue.com

Gütermann
www.gutermann.com

Husqvarna Viking
(800) 358-0001
www.husqvarnaviking.com

Janome America, Inc.
(800) 631-0183; (201) 825-3300
www.janome.com

Kenmore
(800) 349-4358
www.sears.com

Krause Publications
(888) 457-2873
www.krause.com

Loose Ends
www.looseends.com

Me & My Big Ideas
www.meandmybigideas.com

Michael Miller Memories
www.michaelmillermemories.com

Oklahoma Embroidery Supply & Design (OESD)
(800) 580-8885
www.embroideryonline.com

The Paper Catalog
www.thepapercatalog.com

Pfaff
(800) 997-3233
www.pfaff.com

Ranger Industries
www.rangerink.com

Scrapworks
www.scrapworks.com

Singer
(800) 474-6437
www.singerco.com

Sulky
(866) 829-7235
www.sulky.com

White
www.whitesewing.com

Threads from DMC, Gutermann and Sulky.
Stabilizers from Floriani, OESD and Sulky.

Publications

"Creative Machine Embroidery"

Published six times a year. Contains information on machine embroidery, including embroidering fashion, home décor, gift items and paper.

www.cmemag.com

Subscriptions (800) 677-5212; outside the U.S. (386) 447-6318

Back issues www.sewnshop.com.

"Paper & Embroidery" (from "Creative Machine Embroidery")

Special newsstand issue specifically focused on embroidering on paper. Features techniques, projects and scrapbook page layouts.

"Machine Embroidery Essentials"

"More Machine Embroidery Essentials"

Explains the mechanics of embroidery, including the basics of getting started.

(888) 457-2873

www.krause.com

CD-ROM

Instructions

The embroidery designs featured in this book are located on the CD-ROM. You must have a computer and compatible embroidery software to access and utilize the designs. Artwork is also located on the CD if you want to make hand-embroidery or standard sewing machine stitches. You will need Acrobat Reader (a free downloadable software available at www.adobe.com) to view the files.

To access the designs, insert the CD-ROM into the computer. The designs are located in the folders for each embroidery machine format. Copy the design files onto the computer hard-drive using one of the operating system (Windows) programs or open the design in embroidery software. Be sure and copy only the design format compatible with your brand of embroidery machine.

Once the designs are in your software or saved on your computer hard-drive, transfer the designs to your embroidery machine by whatever means you normally use. For more information about using these designs with your software or machine, consult your owner's manual or visit your local machine dealer.

Contents

Embroidery Designs
NOTE: Due to hoop size parameters, not all designs are available in all formats. Some designs are over-sized.

Step-by-Step Projects

Embroidery Design Artwork

ALLOVER	FLOWER1	PDOT3	SCORNER1
BUTTRFLY	FLOWER2	PUMPKIN1	SCORNER2
BUTTON	FROG1	PUMPKIN2	TURTLE1
CCANE	FROG2	RDEER1	TURTLE2
CUPCAKE	LADYBUG	RDDER2	WATER1
DRAGNFLY	LBORDER1	SHOES	WATER2
FLORAL	LBORDER2	SGLASSES	BONUS WORDS: DARLING, EMBROIDERY, FAMILY, FRIENDS, FUN, LOVE, PRECIOUS, PRINCESS, QUILTING, SEWING, SWEETEST
FLBORDER	PDOT1	SBORDER1	
FLOWER	PDOT2	SBORDER2	

Embroidery Design Stitch Information

Machine Embroidery Design Primer

Hand Embroidery Stitches Primer